WOMEN IN HOW MANY CITIES

Duane Vorhees

Contents

ARACHNOLOGIST

My page-spiders
weave their wordwebs
inside your head,
to decipher.

SOCIETY'S SCRIPTS

We live inside our systems of symbols.
A creed, a border, a script for courtship,
we need our ordered dogmas to worship.
Our yous and Is dance to their rituals.

The score is settled. It is all arranged.
(An individual may improvise
within choreography and chorus,
but the rote familiar eases the strange.)

Algorithms determine processes.
The fixed prescriptions neutralize the strains
and routined weather charts predict the rain.
Tested certainties discourage guesses.

We live inside our systems of symbols.
Our yous and Is dance to their rituals.

MANDALAS

The moon woos the maiden waves.
They waver between care and greed,
coyly approach or recede,
as moon acts an inconstant knave.

A worn and generous field
marries the magnificent sun,
and grainy children soon come
who inherit both Daddy's gold
and their mother's charity.

A river surrenders herself,
and her union with the gulf
enlarges her identity.

Maned clouds graze in bluebell skies.
When they're spooked their hooves of thunder
will tear the air to flinders
and waken baby lighting's cries.

NIRVANAMAN

My body is the border
between light and my shadow.

Sometimes I wear the lion,
sometimes the chameleon.

Where is my Nirvana Man,
the one who can quit crawling
among the identities
who inhabit my being?

I am like hostile siblings
hiding inside my human,
senator/saint/assassin.
All drunk on strong wildgod wines.

BREEZES — GALES

My lifetrain went to pieces
when it jackknifed off the rails.

Buddha showed the eightfold path.
I lost it on the freeway.
I had memorized the prayers
but I couldn't do the math.

Some others got the Jesus
but I got stuck with the nails.

TANTRIC ALCHEMY

a.
LUNAR ILLUMINATI

Moonlight albedos
us. We together ourselves,
purified by night.

b.
EROTIC CONIUNCTIO

Our oneness complete,
I applaud stiff rubedo.
The coming of the dawn.

c
DIURNAL REPAIR

Sun's citrinitas
fixes the constituents
nigredo broke down.

ORH

As the sunset swallows the day,
love incorporates identities.

You are the rain
who washes my dust away.

MIGRATORY

I paddled inside you,
my mallard on your pond.
And then *¡away!* I flew.
You waved and waved, alone.

TIDAL

I scavenge driftwood,
shells, and pebbles from the beach.
The ocean beyonds.

WALKING IN A SPRING DRIZZLE

Rain shellacs sidewalk.
Store window mirrors reflect
my dim shadowed face.

LINNAEUS GENESIS

God is existence.
In God's image are beetles,
amoebas, and men.

BESIDE MYSELF INSIDE YOU

I'm old and I'm married
and a thousand miles away.
And yet—

O succubus!
Embrace!

COUNTING THE COCKS IN THE HEN HOUSE

How many celebrants have danced in your penetralium?
Your hangar has sheltered how many planes?

DEPOSITION

Thinking's rearranging information
will displace
thin kings rear-ranging in formation

MY TAILOR,

crisp in his pins and thimbles,
circles and takes my measure.
He garments me by his threads
and then applies his scissors.

EPONYMOUS

Think of the inventions
named for their inventors,
modest benefactors
made by Thomas Crapper

or infamous machines
that victimed Guillotine.

CURSE AND CURE

I am the witch who carries a coven within
and the convict who wears all his prisons inside;
the exorcist who fondles the beads and signs
and the amnesty dangling the keys aside.

THE DAY I FRUIT BASKETED

In morning I wore a peach.
The sun oranged me at the beach.
Evening brought me raspberried.
How fruitful! How varied!

GESTALT

to/get/her
my singularity
we reformed
to/get/her

YOU ARE DECIDUOUS

Your branches in winter
spider like wrinkles.

Where's
your paper birch skin
with its inner pink,
your spring
-leafed hair?

HERE, AFTER

Unless there is a somethingness
I won't even see the black black black

A POEM INDEBTED TO A SERMON BY LUTHER

Banner and anthem. Flag and slogan.
Tattoos and a uniform.

Your circumcision and your tzitzit.
A tonsure and crucifix.

All the princes impose their standards
and propagate their watchwords
by which to their followers they're known
and to which lord they belong.

BELLUM PARTUM

And the whole earth with death and death-cries filled, My Lai,
Might long remember the face of suffering Dresden!
This is a battle hard to endure, and grim. Gaza Gaza Gaza
— Dorothy L Sayers tr *The Song of Roland*

Like zealots
coked on bullets,
the soldiers spread
metal sperm
into harems,
the birth of death.

The bomber
was in labor,
sucked a deep breath,
dropped her load,
her egg of blood,
her birth of death.

THE UNDECIDABILITY IN MIDMOST ME

In my crippledness in your crowd
I split into Solo and Also; in my alone
I bleed between my shadow and my ego.
Our currents are blurred. My substance
is ubiquitous, my components are common.
And still I conceive I'm composed uniquely.
My tide advances ashore withdraws
advances withdraws once more. That which
I have just resolved I then unresolve again.

Can an invisible man still disappear?
Women in how many cities
have unnoticed my presence?

We wish to apportion the What
that's beyond outside into a space,
a time, enumeration, and causality, but
there are not words enough to measure
the random ungoverned imagination,
the divine hunger for enduring novelty.
Yet some of you quest for a wholeness
in which these me cease to exist. I'd
become less than this manyed nothingness.

GUINEVERE AND THE MINOTAUR

"Love is just
an affair
of the tongue,"
you say.
"a poetry."

"But you're wrong,"
I say.
(Nor is it just.
But it's enough
to satisfy
us cold,
us hungry,
us soul-
impaired.)

In our masks,
the cynic's,
the romantic's,
the two of us,
"This, our hour,
our hieroglyph,
is powered
by a myth —
is it a tower
or labyrinth?"
we ask.

LENSES

I was one with those voyeur stars;
I had eyes and thought I could see
through the hollow invisible NotSaids
that keep the planet orderly.

But "Orbit's disjointed!" they say.
I need a new optometrist
"Magnifiers assemble the blaze!
the noose rope already twists!
and our sky's unconstellationed!
we're free to do within our chains!
and we hold too fast to conditions!
we must more dearly count the change!"

So, should I rage
or should I grieve
in my omniscient grave?

STAR ON STAR

your Virtuosa meets my Athlete
where we latch unlatch and latch
we touch on touch
we breath on breath
we wet on wet, with fold on fold
among the night's mighty echoes
ecstatic/static/attic's-tick-tick
each star as perfect as the next
in the vast topless sky
"always" we lie on lie

HORIZONS

Tomorrow's moon
baldandwhite
at horizon
hesitates.

(thunder's hero,
the promise)

Your looking glass
ghosts linger,
your memories
forever
themselves; and each
one's a wave
and each, a beach
that it shaves.

(moonmirror shows
the menace)

Dancing like fire
in the foam,
you're a highwire
thunderstorm!

(horizon's coast,
the phoenix)

Your poemcandle
starts to die.
First it stutters
then it sighs —
our darkhidden
beginnings,
unforgiven
endings.

(yesterday's ghost,
the furnace)

ALL DECISIONS OF THE COMMITTEE SHALL BE FINAL

Your hand is your destiny,
slight or calloused.
So, whether you be an artist
or you be a thief,
no matter where your heart is,
you'll come to grief.
There's a Hanging Committee
for the gallows,
and one for the gallery.

ONCE, I WORE A DELICIOUS FACE

Deltas don't forget distant headwaters.

The bare winter branch no longer flowers.
The butterflies of my youth
have matured into maggots.
That which was garden
has transformed by time's arson;
the glowing bud, the smoldering rose
have become like pollen ash.

To harvest the remaining me
you pearlers must dive deep.

THE RIDDLED UNRIDDLING

Our togethered time was
antic —
anticipation of futured frolic is keen.

Not knowing how becoming comes,
we remained riddlesome.
What wealthy beggars we were!
As innocence succumbed to weariness,
our fountains – they limited;
and foundations – eliminated.

Your footprints faded. I no longer heard your call.

High above all heights,
tiny rags of cloud still cling to sky's naked skin.

Afterwardness knits,
or tears,
pastward threads.

THROWN

I'm being thrown,
knocked into next Wednesday,
but all my bones
are boxed up like hens' eggs.

In my young nest
I dreamed of being bird.
Dreams cannot last
against this cruel, hard world.
I was plucked and packaged
and sold in market aisles.

I'm a javelin
but not a boomerang,
a-hovering
in the air like a hanged
man. I've lost my grounding,
my home is in the sky.

I'm being thrown,
knocked into next Wednesday,
but all my bones
are boxed up like hens' eggs.

BRIDGES WALLS AND DOORS

liars(lovers)(artists)
execute an honest
condemned activity
misshaping reality

art is a seed a hedge
love is a need a bridge
that connects a leisure
to unextinguished torture

greenest seeds weed their way
from criminalities
too covert to commit
and too active to stay hid

the right to scream is held
only by us tortured
the will is a wall made
to support or separate

the corpse is tradition's
usual exhaustion
of palettes and menus
and an unfreedom to choose

love and art are the words
used to mimic or urge
the word is a closed door
but an urge opens the door

ISES MAY BE ISN'TS

It's rape, not sex, unless it is
reciprocal, enjoyable,
spontaneous, and synchronous.

Sabers and foils, not visors, veils —
What we may get's not what we want.
When we need sails we may have gales.

Land that's fragrant's also vacant.
No interval is eternal.
All that's secret is not sacred.

COHABITATION

One's freedom designs one's doom,
and doom patterns one's freedom.

Domesticated as one,
a different damascene
dominates each domain.

One decorates Notre Dame
and one does Nostradamus.

Thingdom is my domicile—
loud energy and atoms,
dumb gravity's domination

YOU ARE MY JACKPOT

I won you on a poker hand.

I thought he thought I was bluffing
so I said, "Double or nothing."

He had two 10s and a 7
and I had two 10s and a 9.

But when he lost he was laughing,
and I didn't see my danger,
I didn't know that I was stuck.

I'm still eager to ante up
to gamble with friends and strangers.
They won't take you as my wager,
so I never have any luck.

THE IMPORTANCE OF WORD ASSOCIATION

Being is the tiger,
an unseen appearance before it swallows you whole.
Seeming is the spider
that builds the mansion where Maya hides the tiger.

And you curl into your spider's blanket and say,
"Yes, there may be other situations. But this one is mine."
These are words of the white sheep that graze on your tongue,
issuing from the edge of your lips to baffle my art.
Belief conceals recognition. Orthodox clichés are sweeter than
exotic heresies.
I need a poet to speak your freedom.

"Poetry!" you say. "That factory of idols! Valueless words strung
together like cultured pearls. A compromise between the universe
and imagination, windy sounds tangled in winter branches. A
sheetless bed in a purple room with no light or exit."

A poem can come from a prophet or a priest or a professor or a
philosopher or a physician or a beautician. But only a true poem
can feel the sun on your face as the snow commandos parachute
in behind enemy lines. A real poem contains stone syllables
standing against a rain-striped horizon.

Let me be your pattern. I've pawned my pasts, demolished the
wall that blocked truth-bearing winds.
To deny my tongue is to strangle your throat.

Together we can be worlds upon a wider world.
Our bronze countenances can besiege the Maya fortress, storm its magic damsel resident therein.
We won't eliminate or lift any veil completely. But we can add invisibility.

"Perception, memory – can't they be real? Who could confuse a long naked body with an artifice of the mind?"
Anyone.
Everyone.
We live in rust on chrome.

"But, that tiger?"

Being is the all-at-once-ness of everything.
The world is not all thieves and wolves. Providers and puppies inhabit too.
Judges and lawyers may be the masters of bar and brothel, and a poem's sentence may condemn. But also it may acquit.
Death is always the same distance away and life as near as we arrange.
Yes, our voyage ends with a wake, but not just the wake behind the boat.

It's now call-and-response time. Your fate depends on your answer.

I say Quiver.
Do you say, "Tremble"?
Or, "Arrow"?

MÖBIUS STRIP

Swans echo the clouds
that echo those swans.

Moon recycles faces, recycles face

I am Today years old, as always
but which we am I taday?

es, recy

This river remembers its geese,
wanders woods in their search.

cles fa

BRIDE OF COPPER

homonyms that mean the same
or, your gray is not my grey

they have divergent offspring
bronze if copper mates with zinc
brass if copper mates with tin

bird as vulture, bird as dove
a painter's silver, or smudge

the flat wilderness of dusk
an opaque landscape of mist

the nothingness of a coin
dime-like or silver florin

hides the man within the war
in a Southern uniform
in a museum's armor

FOUR-BODY SOLUTIONS

*[C'est avec logique que nous prouvons et avec l'intuition
que nous trouvons.* – Henri Poincaré

Indeed, it's by logic that we prove,
by intuition we discover.
To know how to criticize is good,
to know how to create is better,]

Logic. Intuition. And the third
magus offers imagination.
A poetry evolves from a word
by multiplying its dimensions.

Inspiration is the lightning flash
that unshadows sudden eternals
that had been hidden among the trash.
So the fourth horseman is external.

The interaction may be lonely.
Results may be humble as the wedge
or intricate as a symphony.
They may be ignored or widely judged.

The foursome is not always fertile
and indeed may compose a monster,
but their intimacy unriddles
the real and helps edge us onward.

PRE CURSOR POST

Blossom is the baptist
to a fruit called a christ.

Though definitely not moot,
the leaf is not the tree,
nor the branch, nor the root.

The It, not-yet datum,
exists beyond atom
and happens before eve.

The tree has origins
at the Where/When it ends.

FROM VIENNA, THEIR INTERPRETA-TIONS OF DREAMS

Two men fought their Mein Kampfs in their minds,
their unconscious wars on vaginas,
their struggles with a less-than mankind.

While Freud, that Jew, painted Austria
as a vast panorama of dicks,
Adolf Hitler, antisemitic,

bent crucifix into swastika.
Reader of signs, and maker of myths,
these, then, our architects, these our smiths.

GLUE ALL GONE

1. At my touch you'd rain from within.
You'd pulse like pigeons on a bush.

Our stormy passions fused our crows
into a rainbow made for me,
(Monochrome to Technicolor!
Distinguished Valor in a poem.)

Each new day after the havoc,
honored like sabbaths tossed in clay,
ceramic artifacts, intact
(though blackened and scratched) among bricks.

We did love the moon's wallpaper
till stripped by scrapers in sun's gloves.

2. There's a toad between my legs
where I used to rear a snake,
and that nest between your limbs
disintegrated to stems.

3. I was determined to climb the mountains
but you always rode the lifts.
I was eager to dare the uncertains
and you wanted to tame the ifs.

Whenever my compass pointed to lost
you would new-rig my spankers,

and when all meridians were crossed
you would balloon my anchor.

I was the pistol in the crystal shop,
and you the glue in the glue gun.
The day came when you were ready to stop,
though my days had just begun.

You had followed in the wake of my wrecks
with your tender of repairs.
And now I gamble on an empty deck,
my hold bereft of a pair.

YOUR MARRIAGE TO THIS OLD MAN

To possess a stone of rules against those pharaoh-boys
and their noisy persuasions and their handsome toys
you needed to meet a thin christ at Calvary
or a buddha declining in his banyan leaves.

The unexpected dwarf you met your wedding night
was a bullrush baby again, enough of knife
to open a Red Sea but not a Promised Land.
All the commandments are sleeping tablets cut from sand.

You're lost in the desert, and deferred in the dust
your legendary golden calves, your burning bush.

ALL-PURPOSE FACILITY

You were a noted venue
and I would often rent you
for some special attraction.

Equipped to meet any need,
enhance any intention,
sometimes you'd be my circus,
or you'd flaunt a convention.

But my business wore you out.
Now you're vacant and condemned.

HANDS – THEY SHOOK AND THEN...

They futured like gods.
This hand (call it woman),
that hand (call it man)
togethered an applause.

Their fists of spider,
their architect fingers,
built patterns of gauze.

One blob (called embryo)
soon became elbows
attached to hands and jaws
that grew into prayers
to clapclapclap their heirs.

DESCENSUS INFEROS

Our day closes with roses and gold
and soon we'll night
by a river of silver ores
beneath a banner
of christmastree stars
and we'll exchange us presents,
tinsel medallions and
lovingcups of liquid chromium,
and one well will fill another
while, beyond the where-we-are,
your world still worlds its way.
Our tomorrow too will resurrect
in a flamingo and salmon dawn
and then
eventually
end again
in honey and
blood-oranges.

SYMBIONTS

An oxpecker and its rhino.
Lovers in an inexplicable bird cage,
opposites caught despite themselves
in an intimate unity of self and other
becoming other and remaining self.

Strong talons in-digging tough hides
hunting for those hidden ticks
that neverend neverend

However many these lovers may be
they are as trinitarian as time —
a divine Now invisibly linked
to the Not Yet Now to Now No More
becoming self remaining other.

MOSES NEVER WON A NEBULA

Genesis was from the
earliest sci-fi writer,
with tales that told the genre:
A scientist who made
a universe and strove
to keep his androids safe
from any taste of morality
and free from immortality,
and the price the robots paid.
The creation of murder
and the mark it made,
and when the world was drowned.
And divine promises of forever,
transmutations into salt,
and how the nations came about,
and how languages began.
How a prisoner's prophet dreams
unfolded the famines that led
to Pharaoh's favor and reward
and the enslavement that resulted.
He wrote of giants and, later,
of supermen and leviathans,
and how to survive a whale
or a wilderness;
of bushes that talked and burned
and sawing the sea in half
and halting the course of suns.
Some Moses canon is in dispute,
but not his imagination.

IT WAS EVE WHO CHANGED TOMOR-ROWS: A PORTRAIT

Your blonde avalanche threatens to end the temples;
ears vibrate with chants, hymns, and psalms of later rites.
Your eyebrows are branches from the destiny trees.

Your tongue smiles, predicts mankind's ongoing journey
from garden to crypt, from safety to testedness
at Eden's eclipse. Your eye looks to a future
lattice of your ribs guarding mankind's heart,
though they'd been equipped to status your appendage.

Your garter snake lips pulse upon your marble face.
Though angels still dance and geologists still sigh,
your gold avalanche still may bury your temples.

THROWN OVER

Usurped by September,
last summer's emperor
will pass into legend
with his castles of sand.

Days started to funnel
towards autumn's narrow
dark-dominated hours
when the sun would unpower,
the maples would unleaf,
and the winds would turn knives.

You, Queen, deposed August,
saying earth was athirst.
You expect your new king
to provide your sweet reign.
September's rule, so mild,
must soon give way to wild
tyrants whose boons are thorns,
brambles, bitter acorns.

I, the summer's specter,
reminisce my scepter,
my signet, and my orb
while I try to absorb
this flood of banishment.

Once, before you rent
our robes of gold purple,

I ignored life's circle.
It still seems long before
my son's revolt restores.

BLACKENING FACTORY

Magpies harangue
jewelled peacocks
to picket the sky.
The river smiles
        below
                the pier.
The machinery of sex
processes
our progeny.
Silent silver moonface
    ticks
toward overtime.
Dusk goes dark goes dawn goes day goes dusk.

The highway
prays toward
                E N dl es ss s::
perspective. Every exit
becomes
just
another
road

SOME HORIZON

A poet sits next to G. B. Shaw, unopened.
Poet has no mind to drive his pen.
A momentary rickshaw draws from the mist
but is swallowed back in fog with a stumble and list.
Flirtatious Alpha Centauri beckons to the telescopes
but poet's flaccid astronomer fails to focus.
All the usual muses are asleep,
the whiskey and the mistresses, strangers in the street;
neither the etchings on the walls nor the scrimshaw on the shelf
volunteer to help.
Empty poet begs along the Word,
laments poetry's place as kickshaw at the smorgasbord.

And then — poet imagines
Humanity in its dungeon —
unbathed – hungry as a blight —
encaged in rags — in a hint of sunlight —
a detested defiled diseased
tenement for generations of fleas —
the cell's metal, complicit embrace of laxity —
a skeletal thread against a mildew tapestry —
cornucopia of hopeless hope
that even a poor pen surpasses the sturdy rope,
that any desperate continuing
improves on the endless end,
—that hacksaws and pardons
may exist on some horizon,
dandelion the shackles,
and be lion to jackals.

I WEAR YOUR NET

Empires live by iron and corn
and die in marble and famine.
You brought the starvation and war
that harbingered this, my ruin.
I cannot take my rightful throne;
you hold robe and crown and scepter.

All of my ghosts are made of stone.
I'm the quarry, you're the sculptor.

When someone asks me why I wear
your net? I thought it my ladder.

I aspire into stratosphere
but you keep me in your cellar.
My voice and my vision are lost
among your parrots and mirrors.
You use your dust and mist and rust
to confuse merit with error.

LEPIDOPTOURISTS

Folding these my genitals into the soft privacy of the parched cocoon. Careful, Lust! Do not disturb that gentle dust. Lightly, precisely, park your eternal lips against my forever mouth, fasten firmly in place. Yes! Twin thoraces fixed just so! To allow free articulation of limbs in the moon's easy breeze. And, now, our skins unzip along spines, splurge toward the distant vacuum beyond the edge of the linen, until your wings purple lurid under the lunar fluorescence iron themselves indistinguishable into mine (soft-yellowed).

Ahhhhhh. More leaves in someone's unremembered book. All, the rest, is settled. Only our eyes bulge up, multifaceted and questing, from the petrified flatland. Until mourning dawn shakes again the pin loose and fossils rewake.

HAIKU IN SONNET

Blots advertise coming austerity.
Cross farmers and their inner flatterers
spring back into kinetic energy.
Skies are, after all, false benefactors.
(Crows)
"Take careful stock of your remaining fruit,
dead orchards are abandoned and condemned.
Worms sap tunnels through sturdy apple faults."
Home seems familiar. We don't understand.
(to)
The ambitions stretched beyond my quarters,
nests of desires planted over mountains.
Young dreams imagined crisp, boundless borders.
Birds of hope winged themselves across oceans.
(call)
For all that wishful repast was ancient
food that I thought only mine and recent.

Blots cross spring skies: Crows
take dead worms home to the nests.
Young birds call for food.

I, BIBLIOPHILE

One wife memorized Solomon
to reminisce our marriage.
And another remembered Spenser
in bequest to our sons.
And my mistress archived Milton
to remind me of my sin.
If only I'd had more lovers
I'd have read more libraries.

BENEFICE

At my baptism feast
I was immersed
adorned in gown and turban.

The host, swollen with yeast
and drunk with thirst,
cavorted like a merman.

I thrust my jolly priest
into your church
and delivered my sermon.

Hallelujah!

BIRTH-GROWTH-DEATH

We wear our trinity within:
Birth Growth Death.

We place our lots
between these dots:
Birth Growth Death.

Expand the beginning, then end.

Though by zeroes
we are enclosed
—Birth Growth Death—

we still contain infinities.
Birth Growth Death.

ERGO SUM

Smiles spasms and sufferings—
I feel, therefore I am.

Regrets over recent long agos, in the winds and in the sun,
regrets over the lost and missed. Appreciation of some pasts,
nostalgia for the futures.

Wharf odors of salt and gutted fish. Paint and bait, oil and rust.
Clouds scudding overhead, heat miraging up.

Channels changing, the bedlam of soundtrack evolutions.

Limbs and torso shake and stretch, my body hinges into starting
block, toes knuckle against chocks, fingers pyramid on starting
line to lift the earth on edge, ears alert themselves and eyes
ahead; a gunshot accordions our tsunami of feet forward, bellow
elbows explode intense rhythms in lungs and heart like heated
Bismarck batteries firing from iron ribs. And. then. finish line.
Momentum ends, and the broader world returns to regular order
and the runners pant and slow.

Baby's first words and steps, crushes explored and wrecked,
defiance and surrender on every side, alliances of privilege and
power shift from This to Tomorrow.

Geographies of hills and hollows / skin on skin, lips on lips and
nipples, tongue on organ / the old cock and pussy polka to the
strain of gasps and moans.

The Grand Canyon oranging dawn from rim to bottom. Frozen
Niagara's cinder mist.

INHERENT

Your universe is no anarchist,
absolute liberty is a myth.
So cherish the space among those chains.

Infinity also has limits.
So treasure your time in the gibbet,
embrace your inch before that flame.

Though existence may be flexible,
shackles, ropes, and fires are metaphors
for reality's innate constraints.

HUNTERS

My bridge is narrow, but your park is lush.
There is a peril for the ones who rush.

A hundred hungry hunters got lost in your bush,
their thousand-throated thunder silenced by your hush.

There is a peril for the ones who rush.
My careful arrow finds your hiding thrush.

MY I

Moleculed into existence by hope's heredity,
any I is a sum of its actions and its beliefs.

At first these were fostered by practice and authority,
and then in the youth they were constellationed by passion,
and then in a careful age constitutioned by reason.

This nowI lies striated by habit and destiny.

CHANGING HABITAT

That which is between us—
:is it a floor or a corridor?
:is a wall or an interval?
:is it concrete or a ghost?
The cityscape altered,
our promenades became barricades.

Every touch feels more like a cut.
Marathons may falter.
A dozen christenings, one thousand crypts.

All the tears we wept, the saints invoked, the promises broke.
The ends of beginnings.

UNSEASONED

Don't come to me in Yellow,
when thermometers are full
of fever, of sweat, of woe
and nights are by daylight culled.

And please avoid me in Brown.
Environments start to die
and virgin forests ungown
and bare scarcity outcries.

Avoid my presence in White:
Lives lie sleeping in the ground
away from the strangled light,
away from festival sounds.

But in Green I'll wait for you
and in Green we'll reunite.
Green will welcome a rendezvous
between my cloud and your kite.

JASMINE AND COAL

I fell out of the orgasm
that left me bitter and old.
The air was filled with jasmine
but my tongue tasted of coal.

I lived like a revolution.
In the midst of brick and steel
I thought I could find ablution
if I never bowed or kneeled.

I believed only a hedon
was immune to slavery,
misunderstood as freedom
the struggle for ecstasy.

COCOON

I saw my externist today
and got my prescriptions filled
for a well-curated array
of armor auras and pills
to protect me against weathers
and germs. And also to blunt,
like a cuirass wrought of leather,
the intimacy of hugs
and the taste and touch of kisses.
In this invisible plate
I can discover what bliss is,
now that I'm inviolate.

A ROPE AND A PIPE

The sharpshooter's father
learned to dance
when he married the ropemaker's daughter.

"No saddle
instructs the horse to prance.
The lesson is always in the bridle.
Nothing is so efficient as a gun's
violence,"
the marksman taught his son.
"The bullet
can establish your best environment,
find your foe and kill it.
Sing to me when I die
if you wish,
but know that music's a waste of your time.
Don't get drunk,
and put down that damn flute! Be like the fish,
who only dance when hooked."

And the son followed his dad's direction.
A trigger
captained his affections.
But his flute
and humble philosophy and liquor
led him to peace and truth.

MY ABSENT PRESENCE

People will weep.
Maybe they'll pray.
They'll likely say
nice things – Oh, Christ!
—When I met them.
—Where we took care.
—How I look now.
Then all my friends
will become still
as our whole past
binds up their minds
and that's my brand.

ANOTHER YEAR ENDING

The geese are gone.
Another winter's coming on,
and then a sound sleep
before we wake and leap.
Another year's ending,
and then a new beginning.
Because life needs a frame
every year's the same.

DUCT TAPE AND CHICKEN WIRE

A man can fix any part
with duck tape and chicken wire
except for a broken heart
and a field of wheat on fire.
The crop will grow back again
but the heart will never mend.

TONY

My first dog taught me justice,
mercy, and forgiveness.
When I pulled Tony's tail
he bit me without fail,
and then he'd lick my face.
And thus I learned 'bout grace.

God gave a dog to Adam
both as comsolation
and as compensation
for the loss of Eden.

7734

I'm upside down in Hell deeper than a dry well.
Oh, but why am I here with crooked financiers,
blasphemers, murderers, thieves, and adulterers?

The Devil came to me and he grinned wickedly.
"You're here because you failed to live a life unveiled.
You had your mortal faults and kept them in your heart
instead of admitting, instead of correcting.
You, no self-inventor, just let your failings foster.
You never tried to move, get better, or improve.
If you'd been more driven, now you'd be in Heaven."

And then I woke in sweats,
aware of mortal debts.

EXACTLY!

Eggs white, eggs brown.
The yolk is the same,
exactly the same.
Albumen's the same,
exactly the same.
White ones, brown ones,
their soul is the same.

THE SHIP

Oh, the mariner is like the moon;
perfect the once in the month
when my land concedes to your sea.

Our boat was, before, a forest,
leaves like sails, winds
like a petrel's exhale.

Anchored by a stone that once
hugged earth, like mom and son.

And the sea, the sea. The basket
of stars upside-downed, so all
its flowers scatter everywhere.

MY LIFE IN TORNADO ALLEY

—came screaming
through my home
upending everything
in an instant
and then

left
my tattered vacuum
behind, forever—

: the wind and the women

FLIGHT OF FANTASY

The name's Duane, a recovering romantic.
And this sonnet's microcosmically me: intelligent
to an extent, yet unutterably inelegant.
The twisted yogapoetry falls far shy of the tantric.

But the doomed, pure gooneybird still tries liftoff,
flopping/jerking incongruous across your Canada Shield,
this tropical spirit beating its blunt clumsy appeal
against your ever-stubborn massif.

Frantic wings pump and flutter.
Their antics, doubtless, amuse: as awkward
as the balance between golden orator
and the motley's drooling stutter.

The question, then: Can nature's clownbird conquer the runway
and slide into sky's butterandhoney?

INANIMATE ENAMORATA

Pleeztameetyu / whaddyudu?

If I could do anything, I'd love to be your free flowing hair,
the fingertips of my follicles tickling your constant shoulders:
you, praising my full body to the skies—

I'd shear you clear off like a lamb's wool in springtide!

or the palm softened wood of your habitual guitar
cradled into your passionate lap,
neck caressed to perfect pitch —

Even music, I'd gladly banish
if it meant pitching you!

the very odor eaters in your shoes,
if only I could embrace your soul —

But for a day only.
Then bedside
(eagerly coldly)
I'd abandon you
        that's as far as you'd ever get!

then, I guess I'd have to settle on
acting your bathroom mirror,
investigating your secret life
entire—

And I'd shatter your face into diamonds,
just like your illusions,
you peepfuckingpervert tom!

(leaving me in that case merely to wish upon
your vacant genital cavity
your manlacking pussy
handhungry tits,
that the
       gap
             in your ass be as
     empty
as my harmless romantic fantasies—

THOUGHT AND ACTION:
the rise of Brit lit

Pious poets would drink quicksilver despair:
since Creation beggared imagination,
they resignedly would abandon their craft.
But secular old Petrarchus schooled Spencer,
and Shakespeare knew, even while still in Avon,
that, to surpass, he must teach his verse to act.

SUIT FOR EVERY SEASON

One season for clubs, for spades, diamonds, hearts:
one suit for every season.
One card for every week in the year:
each suit has a baker's dozen.

One season for clubs, for spades, diamonds, hearts:
one suit for every season.
One card for every week in the year:
each suit has a baker's dozen.

Stud poker is what we're dealt these cards for:
clubs for the living, spades for the dead,
diamonds for the rich ones, hearts for the poor.

—Hurry up and deal, we all said,
and save the talk for later!

Sailors and gamblers all die between decks,
one suit for every season.
The sailor waits for his day of shipwreck,
the gambler plays for the losing.

—We're dealt such a salty game of paker:
Here's the salt for the baker's bread
and salt for the wet grave of the sailor.

—Just pass the salt, is what we said,
and hold our snack for later.

Lawyers salt their brief times away at court,
one suit for every season;
laws just clubs and spades; they steal the divorced
diamonds, bury hearts with reason.

The dealer shuffles and his hands go blur
and he passes the blacks and reds
and fills our hands with clubs, spades, diamonds, hearts.

—Just deal me wild cards, we each said,
and leave justice for others.

One season for clubs, for spades, diamonds, hearts:
one suit for every season.
One card for every week in the year:
each suit has a baker's dozen.

Stud poker is what we're dealt these cards for:
spades to the living, hearts for the dead,
diamonds from the rich ones, clubs on the poor.

—Just deal those cards, we said, we said.
and keep speeches for later!

MOSQATHEDRAL

(Roma/Mecca amalgaMates)

You bachelors and spinsters:
this Our, O disjoin us not,
identitied opposites.
Our Sames mediate Others.
This Feast of the Unity
of Captive Diversity.
Summers harmonize winters.

LIBIDO THEOLOGY AND DEVELOP-MENTAL STAGE THEORY

Time was still new
in the cooling cosmic stew,
and the immortal prepubescent
was still learning omniscience.

After establishing The Environments
God granted Himself a day of rest.
But, already bored with nascent existence,
He remained experimentally restless.
And so the Creator became the Render
and divided humanity into genders.

But His novel dirt-and-rib mixture
was still a static creature.

And the world still lacked tension,
drama, and dynamic evolution.
So, in order to bestir the universe,
God manifested as serpent.
The event was mankind's catalyst
for stress, embarrassment, and sex.

And while the snake did shed and shed and shed
God, changeless, new-knowing, stayed frustrated.

Though lacking yet any human ego
God sought to assimilate libido.
The divine adolescent jonahed a whale.

But the erotic projection failed:
the prophet was one the whale couldn't stomach.
And soon time exhausted the Tanakh.

And divine anxiety became more urgent.
How could God continue as virgin?
Then God knew Mary and begat himself as Son.
And that's how God became finally human.

SACRIFICIAL

The praying sadist decapitates
her mate
for climax' sake.
"love's addition sometimes subtracts"

The successful huntress offers up
a corpse
on God's doorstep.
"artists always execute their works"

You are that cat,
that mantis
and I the mouse,
the mate.

MENOLOGION

(13 Oct, 16 Jul)

My band played polkas and jazzes
and I soloed on the cymbals,
but then I discovered Jesus
and confined myself to hymnals.

Because Edward the Confessor
presides over painful marriage,
I keep my saint on my dresser
to invigorate my courage.
Supported by my wife's symbol,
I beg from my purgatory.

O, Our Lady of Mount Carmel,
extricate me from my fury.
My old musics live in my feet
and they animate my fingers.
Lord, amputate the Devil's beats,
forever silence the dingers.

EGONOMICS

This I between my left I and my right, Is divided from themselves
by the selves I am not, by the identity of their opposites.
The well of self is narrow and deep, the sky of soul is wide and deeper,
and they are joined by a shallow rain. This is how the All coheres.
The now is the what between hull and coral.
Nothingness is just another existence, a choir that accompanies my
dances.

Among my many ises, in order to anticipate my pasts,
I can see all the futures that used to be.
The present is another sequence of wases and willbes,
a passage between being well and killed, one way from sleep to sleep,
a blurred and fading journal of my vacations and my trials,
of webs and webs of sometimes.

The past has many paths. Life is a flood of poetry: a line of thin rain
followed by lines of sunlight and lines of more rain.
I live within the caesura of my skin but my plural bodies wear
too many faces, store too many heads.

So, I am this uncertain shadow, a stranger to myself,
the corpse between my mes, a confused collection
of doubtful witnesses and contradictory laws.
(Or, rather, though my molecules stay in flux I'm almost always myself
even though I am not the one I once was and not the one I will be.)
I endlessly create myself. I lodge me inside the impersonator I call my
body,
I forge this counterfeit worldly disguise. I never go home with the I I left
with.

My mind is the smithy of all idols. The symbols it imposes
are blankly neutral at the first before they're the crowds of gods.
I've clothed these naked signs with universal aspirations —
for justice/mercy, foreordained free will, for blending all-power to my
desires.
The wise magi found a god in a feedbox; so I can locate mine any where
and then I can exist slowly like mountains, seas, and stars.

I am lived by my genes, beings who incarcerate my existence.
Though the rituals of seduction are usually mutual,
generation nevertheless begins as corruption.
To proliferate this me I need poetry and conception:
I need your body of verses and your erogenous one to unfold and spread
like morning lilies while starlings sing their Sumerian songs.
Then the urgency of the mind meets the wisdom of the flesh,
the cavalry in my entrails encounters the fanatic in your womb.
In the organ dialectic the Old I disappears into a new text.
Thoughts hide inside words and words within thought.
Wordthought erects evolution, poetry engineers environment.
And yet, the poet precedes the poem but is also the product of the page
in the merger of image emotion and happenstance.

My language speaks itself but as a mirror that must reverse.
It fixes and flatters, divulges deceives displays detects distorts,
memorializes my veneration of self-lies, encourages my construction of
shadow.
This is why I confuse reflection with appearance (honesty with vanity).
The All comes in many fashions, styles, and designs.

My cradle is my casket. I am indeed that corpse between my mes.
Everyone lives with death, one of many infinities, though death and life

are both empty phantoms.
Death lives even before birth, and our final death is not life's only one —
and not even its worst. But this instant is my only eternity. So,
dispose of my corpse as you will, with coals or shovels.
The I between my left and my right will unite at last!

But after immortality, what?